W9-CEZ-281

The Red Thread

A Grandparent's Perspective

Grace Braun Upshaw

Deborah —

Thanks for your friendship + support!

Grace

Library of Congress Control Number: 2009939216

ISBN Number: 0-9755188-8-7

Creekwood Press
Lakeland, Tennessee

Printed in The United States of America

I dedicate this book to

Mae Mae,

Uppie,

Grace,

Matt,

Corinne,

Zach,

Curt,

Mary,

And my friend Lynn

Foreword

An ancient Chinese proverb proclaims that an invisible thread extends from the child's spirit and connects those people they are destined to meet, regardless of time, place, or circumstances. The thread may stretch and tangle, but will never break.

Here begins the tender search for a spin in our family's Red Thread.

Decorated flatboat taking visitors to entrance of Summer Palace.

Chapter One

My husband and I have always loved to travel, but our sights had never been set on China—until my daughter and her husband decided to adopt an Asian baby.

After flying sixteen hours across half of the world, we finally landed in Beijing. While our adult children were set on a single intention, our dual-purposed trip combined the pleasures of travel with the excitement of meeting our newest grandchild.

My arms swelled with goose-bumps bigger than hen eggs as the frightening thoughts and feelings began sifting through my mind. Can a grandmother's love stretch as far to the east as this vast ancient land? I was about to find out. Our eighteen-month wait was closing in.

Exemplifying the characteristics of a Baby Boomer, I married before finishing college and had two children within the first few years. Infatuated with being a young wife and mother, I enjoyed cooking and caring for our family while my husband worked to bring home the bacon. We had little, but expected a lot more.

By the time my daughter Grace (her name, in typical Southern fashion, is fourth generation) was in high school, and her brother Curt was in junior high, it became apparent that I desperately needed to establish some independence. I worked part-time at the school Grace and Curt attended as our family went through a few tough and emotional years of turmoil. Eventually, the kids and I moved on.

Grace and Curt were nearly grown and out of the house by the time I met and married Jeremiah, a wonderfully endearing man with three daughters of his own. A remarkable effort of love, patience, and friendship—to which I was unaccustomed—helped our blended family learn to thrive. As we moseyed happily along in our state of marital bliss, I gradually realized one of Jeremiah's greatest assets was being a reasonable thinker while I, on the other hand, was ruled almost entirely by my emotions. Now, after fourteen years of marriage and six grandbabies later, we make a delightful balancing act.

The Summer Palace

Chapter Two

G reeted promptly at the airport by our guide, we were hurriedly ushered through the parking lot to a waiting car and driver. As the four of us sped along the city streets, I realized my nervous apprehension and breathed a convivial sigh of relief; we had made it safely to our first destination.

Hannah, our 28-year-old guide, appeared youthful and extremely laid back, but nevertheless full of purpose. Small in stature and built like an athlete, she was dressed for the heat. Her thick black hair was pulled tightly back into a flowing ponytail enhancing the definition of her lovely round face.

In just a matter of moments Hannah's easy demeanor turned serious as she began to deliver an historical spiel on the first 5,000 years of China, and that was before we made our first stop! We listened to the narration she so earnestly communicated, and I sensed our forthcoming learning experience was sure to be filled with fun and adventure—if, and when, we were able to understand the accent in Hannah's speech.

After checking into the Novatel Peace Hotel we immediately felt comforted by the modernism of the lobby and the large number of Americans bustling about. Hannah waited patiently as we readied to leave for our first site.

The Summer Palace, located in the western part of Beijing, was proudly erected on the grounds of the famous Imperial Gardens. Having been deposited near the visitors' entrance, we followed a massive path of concrete walkways surrounding the venerable enclosure.

The palace, rebuilt in 1850 for the Dragon Lady by the last Emperor of China, sits high on top of a man-made mountain. I entered the roomy stone-walled residence and could hear my footsteps echo through the same hallways once occupied by Chinese royalty more than one hundred years ago. The experience was both awesome and bewitching.

Fronted by acres of Lake Kunming, the effect of the water beyond the meticulous classical garden must have offered a wide range of pleasures for the Queen and her only son. Presently, replicas of colorful sampans and tourist ferries litter the waterway for a delightful departing ride back to the entrance of the compound.

As Hannah described the gardens and palace with pride, I wondered what her parents were like. In what way might their family have been affected by the re-education camps during the Cultural Revolution? Knowing that subject was probably taboo for me to bring up, I decided not to be too inquisitive—yet.

Grace and her husband Matt, a talented artist/plumber, have two children of their own. Zach is a newly developing teenager and Corinne, a precocious nine-year-old. Their ages play a definite role in this story—at least for me.

One afternoon, Grace called to announce the fact that she and Matt had decided to adopt a baby from China. You could have knocked me over with a feather! Thank God I was on the telephone and she couldn't see my face. My first thoughts were, "JUST DONATE MONEY TO THE ORPHANAGE," and "LOOK AT THE AGES OF YOUR CHILDREN." The age thing.

Here entered the conversational black hole. I just HAD to make a sideways comment about how expensive an adoption could be and ended up sounding just like my mother! I loved my mom, but I didn't want to be like her at that moment.

Time stood still as I silently held the phone and hung my head. My heart ached at the thought of hurting my daughter's feelings, but on the other hand, I was so frightened to think of the worry and pain that can be involved with an adoption. Was this really doable from such a long distance?

Selfishly, I was worried about ME caring for another grandchild. Would I take the time to be as involved with their new baby as I had with Corinne and Zach?

What about Jeremiah? He's a wonderful granddad to his grandbabies and mine, but he was my first concern. I had Curt and his daughter Mary to worry about, too.

My guilt was far from the old-fashioned Catholic type. I was born, raised, and remain an Episcopalian, but I continued to come up with excuses for the worry and pain in my heart.

Feeling tethered to the past, my mind flew back in time recalling Grace's maturity as a young girl. We were discussing her upcoming "teenage-dom." I felt compelled to let her know that I might automatically turn into Godzilla, in her eyes, and there was the distinct *possibility we might not be able to talk closely with one another for quite a while.*

My fears of losing this precious little girl disappeared as quickly as time through a keyhole when she adamantly let me know that she DID NOT have to go through puberty like other teenagers. Thankfully, she was right ...and she didn't.

I yanked myself back to reality as Grace was trying to inform me the adoption was a "done deal." She and Matt had worried, prayed, and discussed ad nauseum *every possible scenario, and had thrillingly made their decision. All she wanted and needed was my support. Feeling like a heel, I offered tearful encouragement with a profound apology for having been insensitive to their wishes. Grace comforted me immediately, and once again I was shown the magical beauty of her love and selflessness.*

Tienenneman Square backed by the Forbidden City

Chapter Three

Due to the major time change for Jeremiah and me in China, we awakened way too early and went for a walk along the main thoroughfare in front of our hotel. Having extended our wanderings beyond the shop-filled avenue, we stumbled upon one of Beijing's center city gardens. Only a few short steps away from the slowly rising sun, we encountered some easy trails and began our stealthy trek meandering beneath the cover of trees thick with leaves.

I was gently reminded of the pathways in the luxurious woods on our farm near the outskirts of Memphis. The foreign enclosure seemed to provide the same sense of sweet sanctuary we often experienced while trying to get away from the busy city. Even the earthy smells that penetrated our travel-weary brains allowed us to relish a contemplated memento from home.

We maintained our course and soon stepped out of the gardens. As we approached the street, I noticed men sleeping on benches near the curb and thought, "There must be no city in the world without a homeless population."

When Hannah picked us up later that morning, I expressed my concerns about safety regarding the displaced citizens. She explained that the men on benches were construction workers from the countryside living in the streets near their jobs in order to make money for their families. Embarrassed about my quick judgment of her countrymen, I apologized and became sick with worry that Hannah might think me callous. Obviously, my non-Chinese point of view was showing.

Upon our approach to the sprawling expanse of concrete known as Tienenneman Square, it was easy for me to see that preparations, as in clean up, for the 2008 Olympics were in full swing. The immaculate street was edged with groomed curbs and surrounded on three sides by high modern government buildings. The square held no obvious scars from the ravages dealt on so many Chinese patriots and soldiers, with the exception of a gigantic banner depicting Mao Zedong that was held strong to the wall in front of the Forbidden City.

The eerie calm of the street with the empty cement viewing stands looming on either side of the respectful gate lacked protests at the moment, making it seem as though the student revolution of 1989 *could* not have happened. I later learned that guards are always on call to assure the continued tranquility of the infamous square.

A few questions came to mind as I shivered at the reality of the apparent rather than stated freedoms the citizens may now enjoy. I remained reticent in regards to that subject, realizing the Chinese have certainly come a long way.

Without warning, as if Hannah sensed my inquisitiveness, she opened the conversation about her family and China's planned-birth policy. Born in 1978, she was the youngest of three children. At that time, the rules began to change and, currently, Chinese couples are not allowed more than one child born per family without a prohibitive expense paid to the government for the second.

Many of the big city dwellers are able to afford the government's fees and have had larger families, but it still remains impossible for the peasants; hence the unusually large number of adoptive babies.

Hannah continued explaining some of the variables in the process. If a girl comes first, a family may take the risk for a boy in order to help preserve the family legacy, but, of course, having another girl would involve paying the fee. If an only child marries an only child, the couple may legally have two children of the same sex. Hearing all of the extraordinary information made me realize what hoops the Chinese citizens must jump through, and with that thought, I was mentally reminded of the **real** reasons we were in China.

Feeling more assured that her understanding was forgiving, I asked Grace for the real skinny on their adoption story.

One evening, Matt and Grace were watching Seventh Heaven on television with Zach and Corinne. The episode broadcasted a story about adoption and "The Lost Boys" of the Sudan region in northeast Africa. The content sparked a discussion about families they knew that were helping the Sudanese kids living in Memphis. The subject of adoption had been raised before, but Corinne was always opposed to it.

When the TV show ended, Corinne, concerned that she might be stuck with another big brother, questioned whether or not her parents might seriously be considering adoption. Picking up on Corinne's fears, Grace assured her that the decision to adopt a child would include her in the process, and should that decision be made, they would want a baby, not a teenager.

Corinne was satisfied with the response, but little did she know, their conversation started the ball rolling toward the idea her parents had truly been entertaining.

The very next day, Grace and Matt searched the Internet regarding adoption in China and then watched a video some friends had previously lent them featuring the Holt Agency, located in Oregon. The available criteria seemed to match their needs.

Their search was on.

The Forbidden City

Chapter Four

Our first surprise of the day was a delightful ride in one of the few rickshaws left over from the pre-car era. Both of us sat behind a local young man as he pedaled the two-wheeler, making us feel like the would-be stars of a 1940s "Charlie Chan Visits China" movie as he pulled us through the ancient HuTong neighborhood in historic Beijing.

Tiny alleyways led to old town homes that had been built around miniscule quadrangle courtyards, and we were told that the oldest of these communities was constructed during the Yuan Dynasty.

We ventured down another dusty lane, and I couldn't take my eyes off of two magnificent red-lacquered doors fashioned much like the entryway to a palace. They were recessed from the street on what appeared to be a tiny piece of land enclosed by a nondescript concrete wall. The setting provided a glimpse through the opening into what could have been a gardened compound similar to those we had once seen in San Miguel de Allende, Mexico.

The familiarity associated with the secrecy made me question, "Who might have made that impressive home their residence so long ago *and* under which one of the many Emperors' reigns might it have been occupied?"

Inquiring minds want to know.

Having to forego the comfy rickshaw, the likes of which are not allowed inside the Imperial Kingdom, Jeremiah and I walked with Hannah through the main gate, one of nine entrances into the Forbidden City. Constructed during the rule of the Ming Dynasty, it remains the center of the Chinese world.

Our memorable walk so early on that same morning now seemed lackluster compared to the beauty and antiquity inside the expansive walls. Brightly colored buildings and rooftops literally gleamed with newly replaced tiles and fresh paint.

As we followed Hannah toward the interior section of the Imperial Kingdom, the inspiring atmosphere felt as though the Dowager Empress was still in residence. Each section grew more impressive as twin stone bridges encouraged us onward to yet another living quarter of the dynastic royalty. The more I saw, the easier it was to understand how the city, when occupied, reportedly housed as many as 9,999 people. Oh, but what a dichotomy! Hundreds of tourists were milling about, most of Asian descent, and to think the city was closed to the country's common people for 500 years.

The elaborate residence that contained the stately throne of the Emperor was centered within the massive compound. The oversized windows of the great hall were without panes, which provided the sovereign chair little protection from the weather. I struggled to understand why the government could seemingly allow something that valuable to simply waste away. A replica, maybe? Where might the original be located?

One of the advantages of our tiny group of three was that we were allowed to visit the museum next to the end of the last enclosure. Why it was forbidden to the average tourist was a mystery to us, but we gave Louie, our tour professional, all of the credit for the special treatment.

A countless array of antiquities had been placed in secured glass cases attached side by side with typed cards listing historical data on the front of each—in English no less. I was touched when I realized how fortunate we are to have our language serve as a universal medium.

The kingdom's seclusion made it hard to ignore the fact that thousands of peasants had resided just outside those walls never having had the opportunity to gaze upon such splendor, but merely reduced to hearing the huge city bells of the Drum Towers as they clanged the beginning and ending of each day.

I could hardly liken the terrifying fears the citizens must have had to the irresolute fears I was having about meeting my new grandbaby; nonetheless, my conflicting emotions continued to plague me as each day ticked by.

Will she always be able to gaze upon the multitude of sights available to her?

Will she always be safe and happy in America?

Will I always be accepting of and responsive to her native country?

Will she be as bright and beautiful as her brother and sister?

Will I be able to love her as much as I love them?

Will my love for her always be unconditional and absolute?

And, my greatest fear of all, will she learn to love me?

The nagging thoughts about our new grandchild, combined with my perceptions of the way the Chinese government has forced and continues to force so many parents to give up their babies, pecked sharply at my weary brain.

Fortunately, Hannah with her heavy-lidded eyes filled with enthusiasm thawed my icy spirit as she eagerly taught us more about her country. I realized how lucky she was to have just missed that critical point of separation and had apparently grown up with a loving family. I hated to think about the monumental freedoms and opportunities she may never attain in her country that our new baby will have placed at her feet for the asking, in America, but I knew Hannah would probably remain oblivious to the differences. My foolish heart whispered a silent prayer, longing to keep our new baby from harm, as we hungrily departed the

Forbidden City in anticipation of a sumptuous lunch.

In ancient times, the Chinese people proudly used food as a way of honoring guests in their homes and/or dignitaries in their palaces—the rich always receiving the lion's share. Interestingly, one of Mao's plans of expansion in his notable "Great Leap Forward" produced a massive deforestation in the country, eventually causing the greatest famine on record in human history. But, in the past few decades, the Chinese have made a spectacular comeback with their traditions, for at each of our gastronomical experiences we were generously offered three and four dishes per meal.

Consequently, my mind often leapt back to my childhood hearing my Dad say the old mainstay from our generation: "Clean your plate, remember all the starving children in China."

28

The adoption process was arduous for this sweet family. Once they initiated their course of action with the agency and submitted their intent, a package was received. Included was a form they both had to sign stating their agreement to work exclusively with the Holt Agency. One week later, Grace and Matt received *The Big Red Book* from the agency, complete with all of the steps to follow for the adoption. Their commitment and confidence had prevailed. What a relief.

It took months to fill out reams of paperwork needed for the State, Federal, and Chinese governmental authorities. Even "future" grandparents, aunts, uncles, and friends were required to write letters of recommendation.

For me, I could hardly wait to express what wonderful parents they are, and will be, for one of the true treasures of China.

A section of the Great Wall

Chapter Five

Two more sights were scheduled for Beijing. The first was the Great Wall of China—and GREAT it was!

Astounded by the feeling of reverence I experienced as we approached that bastion of strength built to defend a nation more than 3,000 years ago, my heart wrenched as I imagined the painful, laborious effort it must have required from men, women, and children to construct such a mega-feat of engineering.

Over the decades, thousands of workers had forged forward under the rulers of the Qing, Ming, and Han dynasties as they connected the scattered portions of the wall, gradually producing one continuous structure 4,500 miles in length. Protective beacon/watch towers, strategically placed every fifteen to thirty miles, provided the ability for consigned villagers to signal communities along the wall of any oncoming attacks from their northern enemies. History reminds us that many of the same locales on that rugged highway became centers of commerce that started the inevitable trade route on the road to the West.

Hannah casually led us up the wide, stone pathway of the lower wall. We sauntered much slower than the scads of energetic tourists that milled up and down, many of whom were wearing coolie hats they had purchased from one of the multitude of vendors ensconced along the way.

Gazing out in the distance at the winding, snakelike trail, I noticed the wall seemed to bear a striking resemblance to my mighty Mississippi River that clings to the foot of the Memphis bluff. I was humbled by the thought that each locale encompasses more miles than the eye can see with the same sense of travel and travail.

Consciously trying to absorb the pure unparalleled power of such a majestic vista, I turned to see Hannah talking on her cell phone. The stunning division of past and present worlds, connecting ever so briefly, propelled me back to reality and simultaneously caused a sudden feeling of homesickness.

Not to be outdone by Hannah, I decided to utilize that modern convenience in order to heal my aching and quickly reached out to borrow Jeremiah's cell phone to call Curt and check on the rest of our family in the U.S. Surprised to hear from us, he assured all was well at home, and said he wished his five-year-old daughter Mary and he had shared the trip with us.

It was time to head back to the hotel. Hannah nonchalantly pointed out the way to our car as my thoughts sailed straight to the baby. I wondered, "Could she have northern ancestors that fought against the warring builders of this massive barrier? What if the past generations in her family were born in Mongolia? They were depicted as scary creatures in all of our history books, especially those of Genghis Khan.

"But—surely he couldn't have been all bad. 'The Khan' introduced ice cream to the West."

When our driver turned toward the city, my curiosity made me take one last glance at the largest portion of the eastern wall that still remains today. Built from mortar, stone and brick, it continues to shield the Beijing plain, and, if only in its enormity, the vision made it much easier for me to understand how astronauts are reputedly able to see the Great Wall of China from outer space.

Penny, a local social worker, arrived for her first scheduled home visit with Grace, Matt, and both of their children. After discussing the basics, she carefully explained

the three tracks all of Holt's official adoption paperwork must follow. From Memphis, the dossier would be sent to Nashville (the capital of Tennessee), then to Washington, D.C., and on to the Chinese Embassy in D.C. After leaving the Embassy and going back through the U.S. government, the paperwork would return to Memphis. The file must then journey to the Holt Agency in Oregon before being signed off to China. Whew!!

Zach and Corinne were proud to be included in the process and must have relayed their excitement to Penny, since she made the unsolicited comment, "Their unrestrained happiness was a delightful treat."

As an aside, there was one particular item on the agenda I was happy the children never knew about. The FBI was required to check out their family,,,.scary!

Grace and Matt stayed extremely busy with both of their work places, the children's school and athletic activities, and the weekly mentoring of young-married couples in their church. Even then, with no regard to anyone's sanity, impatience continued to creep its way into all of our lives. The seeming reluctance of the state authorities to proceed made Matt fearful the file lay unnoticed or abandoned on someone's desk in Nashville. So, he made a call to the state representative's office in an effort to nudge the languid process along. I hoped his gentle attempt would make the difference. And it did.

The Temple of Heaven in Beijing

Chapter Six

O ur last stop in China's capital city—the wide, yet limited landscape designated The Temple of Heaven.

Built in its midst was an Imperial sacrificial altar devoted to religious reverence known as the Hall of Prayer for Good Harvest. In the past, it stood as the only building ever allowed to be built at the same height as the Hall of Supreme Harmony in the Forbidden City. Luckily, the altar was spared during the mid-20th century when the communist government destroyed many of the country's lovely temples.

Built in 1420 by the Ming Dynasty, the Hall of Prayer is a masterpiece of engineering as it embodies the craftsmanship and endurance of the Chinese people. Enclosed by three layered terraces of white marble, the circular, cone-shaped hall was constructed without a single nail. Four immense pillars, representing the seasons of the year, with twenty-four smaller pillars arranged in two circles surrounding the central ones, support the richly colored tile dome.

Newly restored to its original beauty, the classic icon stands gleaming luxuriously in the hot sun. No wonder some marketing wizards of the Beijing community chose such an artful remnant as their symbol for the world.

Sitting on 180 acres of impeccable parkland, the Hall of Prayer for Good Harvest provided the perfect setting for the Emperor as he brought his royal retinue to offer sacrifices during the winter solstice.

Today, the grounds remain an oasis of peace. The graceful park serves as a resting place for the city's elderly as they enjoy communing with nature, family and friends.

Grace and Matt had two reasons for choosing to adopt a child from China.

First, they were certain in the knowledge of an above-board process. Secondly, they were guaranteed a baby girl and were aware the baby would come from one of the many peasant families that were the poorest of the poor.

When babies are put up for adoption, the government and/or agency must advertise in the local newspaper to give parents an opportunity to claim their child. As that legal point in time passes, adoptive families can be assured that no one will take their children from them. Thinking not only of themselves but their children as well, that particular part of the process was especially important to Grace and Matt.

Another thought occurred to me. It's always been important for Grace and Matt to impress upon their children the realization that the world is filled with people less fortunate than they, and the need for giving of oneself for another is tremendous. The quest my daughter and her husband were pursuing reflected the admirable traits I so admire in their Christian and American values. Knowing Grace and Matt, when they finally receive their new baby, she will be one of the luckiest children in the world.

Ancient Hutong Quadrangle/Community

Chapter Seven

As part of their total package, all of the adoptive families were required to spend three days in Beijing to visit the sights before continuing the journey on to Guangzhou—the modern name for the older and more familiar Canton area—where the couples were to receive their babies.

We returned to the hotel from our tour with Hannah just as Grace, Corinne, Matt, and their entire adoption group arrived from the Beijing airport. Excitement emanated from the bustling crowd of expectant parents and families pouring off the bus. Once I found my "children" in the crowd, I made a special effort to look at Grace's expression. She seemed okay, so I relaxed a little, then, nervously hugged all three of them. Jeremiah noticed that SOMEONE in our tiny group was just a tad bit edgy. He gently touched my arm and suggested we all go eat dinner at the famous Peninsula Hotel, right around the corner. Everyone was in agreement, so off we went.

The hotel's glassed entrance looked formal and intimidating, but thankfully, none of us were turned away for the lack of appropriate attire. It reminded me of a previous trip to Europe when Jeremiah and I were stopped in our tracks by the stuffy doorman at the steps of a famous hotel... just for wearing tennis shoes.

After riding up a sterile steel escalator, an expressionless waiter appeared and seated us in a small private room decorated with an elongated dinner table, two comfy chairs, and a couch large enough to easily settle three adults. Exhausted from the flight, Corinne instantly fell asleep as she lay between Grace and Matt, while the four of us were elegantly presented with some of the finest Chinese cuisine I've ever had the pleasure of eating.

The paperwork finally made it through the first track. Word came that Nashville was sending the dossier to Washington, D.C. We all were ecstatic.

I was anxious for Matt as I watched him wait for the next step, then, out of the blue, the wildest thing occurred. He was asked to take a volunteer trip to southern China. A small Memphis group had been assembled in an effort to aide a tiny village and Matt was included to help with the plumbing. As the plans architect for his Dad's plumbing company, he was the perfect choice.

Having heard there were limits in place regarding travel to China while adopting, Matt wisely made contact with the Holt agency for the specifics. He discovered the government will not allow any prospective parent to visit an orphanage before the adoption is complete, or the process is negated, money and all. Matt did what he was told and got back home safely to tell his story.

One of four towers on Xian's ancient wall

Chapter Eight

O
ur own three-day tour in Beijing came to a speedy close. The brief visit with Grace and her family passed way too quickly for me, and frankly, I wasn't prepared for the feelings of homesickness that came over me when I had to leave them behind. I knew that we were going to meet up with them in Guangzhou soon, and I actually considered changing our plans, but fortunately, wisdom prevailed. Our itinerary required a precise timetable or we would never get all we wanted to see under our belts.

Naturally, our reservation for the evening train was at the depot's busiest hour. People

44

scurried from the curbside like mice as they chased porters shuffling bags every which way to Sunday. My nerves were still somewhat on edge, so I was easily overwhelmed when we walked into the enormous entrance hall. The multiple arched doors and walkways that were filled to the brim with a convergence of arriving and departing travelers added to the bedlam and noise level, further confusing my thoughts. Desperately hoping not to get lost in the chaos, I grabbed Jeremiah's shirt and held on for dear life as he fearfully endeavored to steer closely behind Hannah.

We approached the confluence of tracks, and I was abruptly reminded of the sinews in a muscle man's arm as the endless railways entwined one way and then another. Finally having located the correct platform, Hannah gave directions to our heavily burdened porter who had, by the way, miraculously beaten us to the train car.

Subsequently it was time for our departure, so we quickly reached out and hugged our enthralling new friend. Jeremiah slipped her a healthy tip, and both of us thanked her for the marvelous tour and climbed anxiously aboard.

I giggled as we watched Hannah quickly disappear in the midst of the hubbub. She was dressed in her daily uniform of black Capri pants and a white blouse and, certainly no surprise to us, she was already holding her cell phone closely to her ear.

GREAT NEWS!

The official paperwork returned from Washington, D.C., signed and sealed by Ms. Condoleezza Rice, the United States Secretary of State.

Grace and I work in different capacities at a Christian elementary school that's comfortably surrounded by the campus of a large mid-city church. Matt called us when he received the papers and brought them by for

Grace and me to eyeball the famous signature that consummated the touching process. I was thrilled for being included in the excitement, and quietly gave thanks for the surreal new world exposing itself to my family and me.

Matt wasted no time hitting the first post office he could find in order to return the file back to the Holt Agency. At that point, I once again began to dread the next interminable wait they must courageously endure...the date the dossier should be sent from Holt to China.

Ancient stone wall in the city of Xi'an

Chapter Nine

Jeremiah and I quietly settled down in the private coach for an over-night train ride to one of the ten largest cities in China. Xi'an turned out to be every bit as fascinating as Beijing.

Upon our arrival, thanks to our illustrious tour planner Louie, we felt confident once more as we saw a sign bearing our name, held by Kelly, our new guide. I had to chuckle at another Americanized tour guide's "handle." Smaller than Hannah, Kelly seemed fragile with her slight, trim build. Her large round eyes and humorous smile were gently framed by unusual blondish-red hair.

Noting her behavior exuded a more sociable outlook as she delivered our second history lesson, I decided the culture of Xi'an made the difference in the two young women, until Kelly mentioned her husband. It was then I understood her maturity.

Right off the bat, we were treated to a cafeteria-style breakfast and hustled toward an ancient section of Xi'an that had been enclosed by a massive wall of stone many centuries ago.

The driver was compelled to bypass two of the four blockaded gates before stopping just long enough to drop us off in front of the southern gate tower that contained Xi'an's old-city museum. Chocked full of information and complemented by hundreds of honorably placed remnants of the 14 dynasties, the exhibition roused our interest. After I peeked inside a well-stocked gift shop to buy a small memento, a young female docent requested that we both take a seat in the room next door to hear her delivery on a brief history of Xi'an. She continued to reel off information while simultaneously motioning us to follow her up a short flight of stairs. There we were introduced to a magnificent waist-high half-horse/half dragon made of jade and marble that stood proudly facing down the steps leading to the front doors of the building. That mysterious animal gave way to yet another concise lecture, on *fengshui*. We listened with interest, patted the secretive dragon for luck, and walked down the stairs and straight out of the solid iron doors.

The CCAA, China Center for Adoption Affairs, in Beijing was the next stop for the meandering dossier. Once translated, the officials would finally match a baby to Grace, Matt, and their family.

It was hard to define the frustration that continued to overcome me as I allowed what I perceived as the Chinese government's style of processing get under my skin. Some of my anxiety might have been the result of stress caused by the length of time each step the adoption was taking, but it was more likely from watching my sweet daughter and remarkable son-in-law sit on pins and needles in anticipation.

The dreadful wait reminded me of the night Zach—the first grandchild for all the in-laws and out-laws in our family—was born. Grace, in her delicate condition, called to inform us that her water had broken, so Jeremiah and I left in the middle of eating dinner with friends and hurriedly met her and Matt at the hospital.

For six long hours I was filled with feelings of anguish and empathy as I held on to the chair at my daughter's bedside. My strength, seemingly super-human to me, started to wane around eleven. It was nearly midnight by the time Grace, in her medicinal haze, realized the date was April 1st. She became unrelenting and held on a little longer, vowing there was no way her baby was going to be teased about his birthday for the rest of his life.

I was floored at the thought of trying to put off the inevitable, but, in any case, Grace's utter determination won out. Zach was born on the 2nd.

Passengers riding in golf cart on pathway of ancient Xi'an fortification.

Chapter Ten

Kelly championed the importance of *fengshui*, which literally translates as windwater.

Believing inexplicable factors are involved, many still hold true the superstition and consider it a metaphysical art. In ancient times, *fengshui* was known as the Law of Heaven and Earth. The docent from the museum had described it as a technique of properly placing physical objects to achieve a cosmic harmony with the environment. As Jeremiah often says, "It sounds like people with too much time on their hands."

Having pointed out primary examples of *fengshui* were usually found in construction of Chinese architecture, Kelly added the fact that developers continue to build homes and offices with a backdrop of mountains or taller structures combined with frontages that boast waterways, fountains, or rivers to assure hopes of maintaining their prosperity and good fortune.

Finally filled in on some of the mystery, we continued our tour of the ancient capital with a rigorous climb up steep concrete stairs that led to the fifteen-foot-wide stone walkway encompassing the 950 year-old wall. Out of breath, the three of us put our elbows on the waist-high circuit and gazed at the panoramic view of old and new Xi'an.

The original stone walls protected the historic city by connecting its four towered gates, like signs on the posts of a weathervane, each facing in opposite directions. Impeccably repaired, the ancient path was perfect for enjoying a morning ride in an oversized golf–cart.

Sitting comfortably, we listened to Kelly give another history lesson and imagined the enormous entourages that must have promenaded along that very spot. One hour later, the blistering heat became overwhelming as our transport continued along the concrete. Thankfully, we encountered some enterprising vendors handily selling bottles of water at a fairly modest price. Thirstily, we made the purchase and at the same time appreciated the modern convenience, knowing it would take a little longer to complete the ancient passageway.

After stopping the cart to peer over the side, we longed to walk through part of the historical inner city, but the modern apartment buildings and original pagoda-style townhouses were being refurbished and were apparently off limits.

Once again—with the novelty of freshness tied to thoughts of tourism—everywhere we looked the signs of preparation for the upcoming Olympics were confirmed, making it obvious the Chinese had outlaid another bundle of bucks in Xi'an.

On the ride to lunch with our driver, Kelly told us a cute myth about pagodas. The belief was, long ago there were dangerous dragons living below the earth. Pagodas were built over the entranceway to the dragons' caves in order to keep them underground. If the pagoda should fall, the dragon would be free to climb out of the ground and wreak havoc on the community; hence, the revered position pagodas still hold.

That might frighten our newest grandbaby. We'll have to wait a few years.

Knowing the adoption was closer to reality, I asked Jeremiah if he might want to consider visiting China while Grace and Matt were there to get the baby. He loved the idea and expanded our options much further than I anticipated.

Next, I went to Grace and Matt's. I preferred talking face to face so I could see them flinch if they did NOT want us to go. Timidly, hoping to appeal to Matt's love of travel easily equaled to ours, I began with our thoughts of visiting China and explained our idea was to tour six cities, but the catch might be in the timing—for them. As I laid out our plan, I asked would they be bothered if Jeremiah and I were in China the same time they were to be there for the adoption, quickly adding we would certainly try to be considerate with regard to their personal time. We did not want to butt in, but wanted to schedule our visit in Guangzhou for a few days after the baby had acclimated to her new family. As a caveat, I also encouraged the thought that it might be comforting to have family nearby—as in the same country.

Grace's face lit up as Matt smiled. I knew we were in.

One small section of the terra-cotta soldiers museum

Chapter 11

The chances of seeing one of the most powerful sights in China had evoked such excitement for Jeremiah and me that we could hardly contain ourselves. Kelly was taking us to the museum that contains the renowned terra-cotta soldiers, clearly one of the most incredible highlights of our trip.

The entrance of the park simulated Disney World as lines of tourists walked through the maze of handrails that guided everyone toward a block of ticket booths. On the opposite side, vans were parked with drivers standing by, ready to take visitors for a short ride through the newly groomed park that led to the enclosed pits containing the famous treasure.

In 1974, a local farmer was drilling on his land and up popped a strange-looking head made of clay. Luckily, archeologists were promptly called in and soon discovered that the farmer had stumbled upon the grounds of a 3rd century B.C. replica of ancient Xi'an. Additionally, in close proximity to the original site, was a separate, grass-covered mound yet to be entered.

The underground city had been constructed under the rule of Qin Huang Zhe, the military-minded Emperor noted as the first ruler to have united the six provinces of China and to have established the country's first common currency.

Inside the massive gravesite, an enormous field of 8,000 terra-cotta soldiers was uncovered. All stood in battlefield formation along with their horses. The life-sized warriors were dressed in full ceremonial garb and armor, with sculpted faces holding true lifelike expressions. The well-disciplined army was surrounded by carriages for chariots and priceless bronze weaponry of war, some even "chromed."

Today, thousands of pieces have been restored by hand to reflect their original color, then delicately placed back into formation. But, scads of the terra cotta still lie untouched, covered with centuries of dirt and debris. Scholars, archeologists, and artisans from China and all over the world remain at the site to continue their tedious jobs.

A newly built protective platform surrounds the ancient military force enabling the public to walk reverently above the bedrock and to read each vista point describing the alluring soldiers and life-like steeds as they are meticulously transformed.

Presently housed in three gigantic pits larger than four football fields, the amazing find is encompassed by the Qin Shi Huang Museum, assuring prolonged safety from plunder, as well as protection from the weather.

About 4,000 years ago the powerful gravesite was closed upon the death of Qin, but the harshness of the Emperor continued. Reputedly, the forced-labor construction workers that built the sepulcher were buried alive to forever safeguard his hidden memorial.

Qin's entombed remains still lie inside the enormous mound near the museum and have apparently never been disturbed. It's easy for me to imagine the media waiting like wolves at the door for the day the government allows the covered grassland to be excavated.

Having settled on the prospect of taking a trip to China, my concern for Corinne's welfare while Jeremiah and I were to be gone, became paramount in my mind. She was supposed to have stayed with us while her parents were traveling to get the baby.

Obviously, that plan was no longer in the cards. Zach had chosen to go to camp at the same time all of us were going to be out of the country, so I could hardly allow myself to leave Corinne behind. I decided to try my luck one more time and ask Matt and Grace about the possibility of taking "big sister" on our life-changing adventure. They happily accepted the proposal. With a second nod of approval, I was finally content with all my little ducks in a row.

As the preparations for Corinne's passport and visa were quickly put in order, Jeremiah and I decided to contact Louie, the dedicated travel agent who makes all of the arrangements for the Holt Agency. We asked him to focus on the cities that piqued our interest, and to place Guangzhou, the spot where we were to catch up with Grace and the baby, toward the end of our itinerary.

Signs of sharing our lives with the newest member of our family were growing stronger and stronger.

A terra-cotta chariot among the soldiers at Xi'an

Chapter Twelve

For our last morning in Xi'an, Kelly's organized agenda led us on an informative tour of a busy cloisonné factory located next to a towering mall filled with various manufacturing facilities. I was fascinated as we walked through a room full of male and female artisans seated at long worktables, patiently hand-painting intricately detailed looped designs engraved on multi-sized ceramic figurines.

We learned the myriad shapes had been previously lined with thin sheets of copper and baked in a kiln. Then they were ready to be worked on by the artists. After the professionals completed their task, the pieces were fired once more to produce a lovely finish.

Upon leaving the workers' area, we were led into an enormous showroom with an exhaustive amount of finished cloisonné ceramics, wrapped and ready for purchasing. What a tourist spot! For me, it was the perfect place to buy special gifts to take home for our family and friends.

Subsequently the three of us entered the building next door and wedged ourselves into the showroom of a pearl factory. It was packed to the gills with tourists closely accompanied by their guides. The non-locals were practically drooling over the professionally arranged wares that longed to be bought, making it almost impossible NOT to acquire a pertinent purchase.

My head swam as I scanned the room and ogled the untold amount of cultured pearls displayed in every imaginable fashion. I noticed Jeremiah cringe as he watched dozens of sales people with hope on their faces as they attached themselves to "clients", and dreamed of healthy commissions. He silently resigned himself to the fact that we were probably headed in the same direction and, of course, I didn't let him down. Together we picked out five unique large-pearl bracelets for all of our grown-up girls.

We were ready to depart Kelly's magnificent city when she decided there was just enough time for us to experience one last and, as she put it, "unusual" meal together.

I became a little reticent when we entered a huge convention hall filled with attendees of what appeared to be a mid-day wedding party, engaged in a celebratory meal. I promptly eased as Kelly guided us away from the festivities toward a corner in a less obtrusive area.

Sitting in the middle of a reserved table was a huge black kettle supported by a low wrought-iron grill. A small gas fire underneath was hard at work heating a dark, strange bubbling concoction. I noticed a number of long pointed skewers and a large platter filled with chopped food that accompanied the table setting. It slowly dawned on me what we were about to enjoy.

The famous trendy fad of the 1970's in America.... fondue!

Could this really be an ancient Chinese delicacy the French named and claimed as their own? Whatever—but, I say, when in China...

Kelly called it a "hot pot'" as she offered us a seat.

Greatly reassured about the meal, I helped Kelly carefully drop the raw vegetables and meat into the kettle of boiling oil. While all of the food simmered, we sampled the exotic dipping sauces that were served in tiny bowls and placed indiscriminately around the table.

We nixed the weird flavored ones, filled our plates with the cooked veggies and meat, dabbed a little sauce on each piece, and hungrily devoured the tasty repast while Kelly described a typical wedding in Xi'an.

Qin Shi Huang Museum, which houses the terra cotta soldiers

Getting to know our second Asian friend certainly made us feel more at home in China, but we still had such a long way to go on our real pursuit. The different personalities and inherited traits of the two young women kept forcing my mind toward thoughts of the baby. What will she look like in person? Will her eyes be small and more slanted like Hannah's, or large and round like Kelly's? Will she be stocky and short, or thin and willowy?

The closer to Guangzhou we traveled, the more I became consumed with thoughts of her. Each time I saw a baby in her mother's arms, I desperately wished I were holding our new baby. Every little girl holding tightly to her mom or dad's hand made me wistfully dream about gently grasping my own new granddaughter's hand.

Anticipation had nearly overwhelmed me when, just as we were prepared to leave Xi'an, Jeremiah's cell phone rang. Grace was calling to let us know that she, Matt and Corinne had just finished their tour of the required sights on their Beijing schedule and were anxiously awaiting the plane ride to Guangzhou. Impulsive tears slipped from my eyes as I heard her longingly whisper, "One more day and I'll be holding our new baby."

An old phrase my grandmother used to say suddenly slammed into my brain. I felt like a bull in a bog as all of us remained in the same pattern of waiting for our precious treasure so close, and yet, so far away.

Jeremiah and I received our tentative itinerary from the ever-efficient Louie. The incredible list of cities we hoped to visit seemed mind boggling; Beijing, Xi'an,

Shanghai, Guilin, Guangzhou, and Hong Kong. The trip of a lifetime was only a plane ride away.

Indeed!

The demand for last minute arrangements made it necessary to constantly check the airlines for flight availability. Matt and Jeremiah wanted their frequent flier points to garner at least one of their overseas tickets needed.

Frustrations mounted as all of us were left in limbo for nearly two months...waiting for the official timetable from China.

The Oriental Pearl

Chapter Thirteen

When we arrived in the cosmopolitan city of Shanghai, our luck held out. Jo Ling, our stunning new guide, was waiting patiently at the gate. Tall and very slim with long black shimmering hair, she exuded sophistication.

Busily visualizing how she might have looked as a baby with her creamy, almost iridescent, white skin and bountiful lips, I was barely to return from my digression in time to hear Jo Ling's soft voice impart our first mental picture of Shanghai.

With 16 million inhabitants, there must have been an equal amount of cars and bicycles as our new driver professionally maneuvered his

Mercedes through the city. Horns blasted like pepper spray, humanity cluttered every intersection, and the crowds walked and cycled in hoards as they tried to bypass the manic automobiles and taxi drivers. I was a nervous wreck until we stopped in a cozy neighborhood thickly enveloped by a copse of trees.

Tucked behind an expensive wrought iron gate was a chic hotel. Louie had made our reservations at a villa replicating one that might have been plucked right from the countryside of France. The driver pulled into the narrow turnaround as an imposing doorman stepped out to open our door and gallantly usher us into a splendidly appointed parlor.

I stopped to appreciate each charming nook containing black enamel chairs trimmed in ornate gold leaf, and to take note of the impressive oil paintings gracing each wall. As a result, having fallen behind Jeremiah as he walked ahead into the lobby, I found him relaxing in an attractive and "manly" chamber that was slightly recessed from the elegant reception setting.

The barroom featured several handsome chocolate-brown leather chairs and a few cozy tables previously set with a service of delicate Limoge, sitting in wait for afternoon tea. As I took a comfortable seat next to Jeremiah, I could smell the pleasant, spent fragrance of lingering pipe tobacco as it hung lightly in the air.

A grandiose walnut registration desk stood ready for Jo Ling to check us in. She did so and led us upstairs to a luxurious suite fully equipped with all of the extras, including personal maid service. She left us for the rest of the day, allowing our surrender to a much needed rest.

Early the next morning, Jeremiah enjoyed a continental breakfast downstairs in the formal dining room. He sat at a small table and was joined by a gentleman from Denmark. The man imparted that the hotel generally catered to businessmen and added he had been staying there regularly since 1996. He continued with remarks on his company's financial growth and opportunity comparisons in China then and now, and informed Jeremiah about a variety of new business ventures that were inundating the Chinese market.

He stood and parted company with one last and most enlightening statement,

"The economy of Shanghai makes more money than the entire country of Holland."

The Holt Agency contacted Grace and Matt by telephone to inform them the Chinese Embassy had received and processed their referral. The official adoption paperwork should arrive in the following day's mail.

Thank Heaven, it did. They had forty-eight hours to respond with their confirmation and, of course, not a moment was spared. Details in

the packet also specified that a Fed Ex package would arrive in a day or two, and enclosed would be a picture of the baby, and, an approximate time-table for their departure date to China.

The following day, a delivery person rang the doorbell and held a next-day-air letter in his hand. Anticipating the contents, the children followed Grace and Matt out onto the porch and inundated the poor guy with hugs and squeals. Upon hearing the commotion, Grace's neighbor came outside and was quickly handed a camera to take a picture of the four of them with their new friend standing proudly in the middle of the excited throng. A little embarrassed, Matt apologized for the craziness.

The delivery man responded by saying, "Don't worry. I know it's hard to believe, but you and your family aren't the first ones to receive adoption papers from me."

With that, Grace handed him a candy bar that was specially ordered and printed with the baby's name on the label. He waved goodbye with a huge smile on his face.

For the next hour, Matt's cell phone burned with excitement as he alerted the entire family of the thrilling news. Everyone came right over, including the rest of their neighbors, to join in on the celebration.

With a dozen candy bars in their hands, Grace and Matt announced to all of us the name they had picked out for the baby. Zach and Corinne had heartily agreed—Sarah Mae was on her way!

Sarah was the name of two Chinese Christian women Matt met on his previous visit to China. Plus, Matt and Grace liked the name. Mae is the name of Matt's grandmother. And, Matt and Grace liked the Chinese meaning.

Mae Mae in Chinese means little sister, and Mei also translates as beauty and grace—close enough for me!

Chapter Fourteen

Developed by power, not by design, Shanghai led the economic revolution, and remains its own separate economy from the rest of the country. As a seaport in eastern China, near the mouth of the Yangtze River, it contains a critical view of the present and past.

Seated on both sides of the Huang Pu River, Shanghai claims an older Colonial hillside constructed during Britain's heyday in the early 20th century. Stationed majestically along the busy roadway is one of the three iconic Big Ben clock towers that were built and placed around the world. London boasts the original, with another present in Moscow's Red Square.

After our short tour of the city, Jo Ling and the driver dropped us off for a stroll along an embankment near the riverside, aptly named the Bund, where we watched the ever-universal entrepreneurs hustle their wares to the unassuming. Of course, I quickly got sucked in and bought four pairs of skates easily attachable to the bottom of tennis shoes. They were heavy, but the grandbabies would hopefully appreciate them.

About fifteen years ago, a former farm across the river from downtown was bulldozed and filled with magnificent high-rise office buildings, hotels, and condominiums, thus creating the famous financial district now known as Pudong (Pu means river; Dong means South). Visitors have recently been given the opportunity to reach the skyscraper region in just a few short moments via a brand new magnetic levitation train from the airport.

Jo Ling's printed itinerary stated a boat ride had arranged for the next day, so we grabbed a snack and headed back to the hotel, looking forward to an effortless evening of relaxation.

The tallest building on the same side of the river, Jin Mao Tower, is a lofty 40-floor Hyatt Regency Hotel with business offices on a few of the lower levels. It looked quite grand from our view on the boat ride around the harbor, but there were no opportunities for us to disembark and venture inside.

As we traversed a little farther around the bend in the river, the famous Oriental Pearl stood shimmering like a beacon in the sun; an elegant TV tower shaped like an old-fashioned Christmas ornament or a spaceship, familiar around the world as the marketing symbol of Shanghai.

When our afternoon cruise ended, Jo Ling instructed the driver to take us back to our hotel. From there Jeremiah and I walked to a busy avenue lined with shops and restaurants. Prominently placed in the middle of the block was a TGI Friday's bar and café. Overcome with delight at finding something so familiar, we marched straight in and enjoyed our first hamburger in weeks.

As I thought back on our day, the farmland transition of Pudong reminded me of the fields south of Memphis in the Mississippi Delta. Amidst all the cotton and soybeans sits Mhoon Landing of Tunica, a casino Mecca. The seemingly similar communities were both constructed in the middle of nowhere, and were recently filled with young employees laboring over computer-driven hardware on tabletops groaning from the weight of other peoples' money...at any rate, that's the way I see it.

I had just returned from our farm when the telephone rang. As I answered it, I could hear a faint sigh of relief in Grace's voice as she told me they had just received a picture of the baby from the agency. I went straight over to her home.

The photographer had Mae propped up on a huge white pillow and wrapped in a fluffy pink jacket. Mae's expression was emotionless, not even the hint of a smile as she stared at the camera.

It was impossible for me to determine her size, and in that get-up, I was concerned she might be freezing in the orphanage.

I tried to commit Mae's face to memory and wondered how all of the families must feel as they received the same type of posed pictures. I watched Grace, and her trust seemed to gain momentum as she sensed the promise of a healthy child, but my emotional thoughts about the machinations the Chinese government seemingly manifested while picking babies for prospective parents, made a few incensed feelings return with vigor. Fortunately, my negative mental attitude abated as soon as I realized there must be some sort of order in the chaos of choosing.

Dare I hope that Mae was being lovingly cared for at the orphanage? In my mind, I knew there weren't enough caregivers for that possibility, but in my heart I preferred to feel she was safe, warm and nurtured.

Overwhelmed with sadness for all of the children without parents, I startled myself as I understood Matt's often repeated comment: "How do we take just one?"

With a new wave of heightened consciousness, I felt the tremulous twinges of a grandmother's love and joyfully allowed gratitude to take over. Those fearful thoughts I had harbored earlier in the process were beginning to fall by the wayside. I grabbed that moment to earnestly thank God for the start of amazing changes in me.

Yu Yuan Gardens with reflecting pool in a luxurious lagoon

Chapter Fifteen

Jo Ling picked us up early the next morning for a visit to the Shanghai Museum, located in the center of downtown. Four artistically designed floors were filled with exquisite historical pieces of the city; water colors and oil paintings depicting modern and ancient China, priceless examples of Ming and Ting pottery, jade, bronze, and a marvelous display of historic calligraphy.

Not far from the museum we strolled toward another historic landmark, the Yu Yuan Gardens, built 400 years ago by the Ming dynasty. After the turn of the 20th century, the home and gardens were acquired by a Chinese family who later encountered financial ruin and allowed the city to take the property over for tourists to enjoy. A small canal continues to trickle through the gardens pouring into a reflecting pool located near an aged and priceless pagoda still filled with original furniture made from an ancient banyan tree.

Always appreciative of the chance to enjoy a new food experience, we noticed it was time to eat. Every restaurant on the harbor was filled with young businessmen and women focused on the financial and professional pulse of the city, each vying for a bite out of the new economy. I felt sure our lovely guide was included.

We enjoyed a typical four-course meal in a small café located close to the energetic waterside. The talk of commerce brought us to another subject. Jo Ling began discussing displacement of Chinese family life. I understood her to say the older generation was slowly being pushed out of their smaller homes in the city and relocated in newly built concrete high-rises on the outskirts of Shanghai. As a result, the young adults were spending less family time at home, opting instead to search for the realms of opportunity and fortune in the big city.

Listening to Jo Ling, I was amazed by the similar family situations in China as compared to those in the States. Many young people seem to be allowing core beliefs go by the wayside in order to clamor after the ultimate buck. Not wanting to sound critical, I refrained from comment and contemplated the positive impact prosperity has made in the world.

Mao referred to his takeover as liberation. He should see what capitalism has done!

It had been exactly six weeks since Grace and Matt had received their referral. The Holt Agency contacted them again. Mae was to be

delivered on the 25th of June, one day after her first birthday. We all scurried to secure our plans.

I could scarcely believe sixteen months had passed, and yet, it seemed interminable. Summer was scratching at the door and the school year was coming to a close. Our headmaster made an announcement at the last faculty meeting that Grace would not be returning to teach the next year. She stood and excitedly explained the happiness about to occur in her family's life, and proudly passed around her only picture of Mae.

The quality of our lives is known to be determined by our relationships. I felt more than honored to be included in the attainment of our newest family member.

A boat carries visitors through an ancient water- town's canal

Chapter Sixteen

Jo Ling escorted us through an elegant park located near an ancient open-air opera house and pointed out with a sense of pride the exact spots where such luminaries as President Richard Nixon (often accompanied by his U.N. Ambassador/Envoy to China, George H. W. Bush, noted to have been innovative in American/Chinese relations) and President Bill Clinton had delivered speeches during their famously photographed visits. I found Jo Ling quite enamored with the latter, and I wasn't particularly surprised by her admiration. I felt as though the Chinese regulated governmental TV stations, and the world in general, probably showed only the popular portions of his presidency that were consistently aired by the American news media.

An hour later, we rode quite a distance out into the countryside for a visit to a 1000-year-old water town. Refurbished for tourism in the last 15 years, the village sits nestled on a Yangtze tributary that formerly served as the only viable connection to Shanghai for most of the farming communities.

The old governmental road system built highways skirting the smaller towns, making travel and prosperity more difficult. The only option left for them was to load their produce onto small flatboats for transport into the city. Of course, currently that type of trade is no longer in practice, but many of the villagers still fish as their ancestors did, with the daily catch dependent on the weather.

The water towns were constructed with small stone bridges for crossing over the canals and for connecting the multi-walled alleyways on either side. Each alleyway had diminutive homes facing each other and were adjoined by thick stone walls.

Interspersed along the canals were specialty shops for selling clothes, "gourmet" foods, souvenirs, and most delightfully—especially for the two visitors steadily enthralled with eating—a few choice spots for neighborhood cafés.

In quite the timely fashion, Jo Ling led us to a quaint eatery that displayed an open-air window facing out toward the canal. We were seated just as our stomachs began to growl in anticipation of another yummy feast.

We weren't disappointed. The first course of our lunch consisted of a spicy chicken dish covered with roasted peanuts. The second course was a small dish of juicy beef combined with typical Chinese vegetables. But neither could compare with the third, which was definitely my favorite. A small portion of delicious pork ribs had been individually wrapped in reed leaves and tied with string, covered with a delicious homemade barbeque sauce, then slowly cooked over a low coal fire for a couple of hours. They were absolutely to die for as they melted in my mouth. Instantly I thought, "What a hit these ribs would make for the Food Channel!" I even considered the possibility of trying to figure out the same type of recipe for our cooking team back home that participates in the Memphis in May International Barbeque Cooking Contest.

Jo Ling appeared a bit worried when I got carried away with the excitement of trying the delicious ribs again. She quickly let me know the type of food we'd just enjoyed could not be found in the city. Man, I sure hated to hear that.

After lunch, we walked through the tiny village and watched Asian tourists enjoying scenic rides in old fishing boats. One group floated along the canal smiling and waving as they steadily snapped pictures of us! What a hoot.

We walked a little further down the riverside and noticed a family of four kneeling next to the water's edge beneath one of the ancient bridges that linked the community. Enthralled with watching one after the other pour live goldfish from a baggie into the water of the canal, I looked inquiringly at Jo Ling.

She explained the parents were active Buddhists teaching their young children how to place their prized purchases into the water beneath the "living kindness bridge." She added that Buddhists believe when nice things happen to them, they should return a living kindness back to Buddha as a sign of gratitude.

Then Jo Ling began to explain that Buddhism is a belief in life's circular cycle. The Chinese word for gold translates as money, and the word for fish sounds like their word for surplus, thus finally defining the donated gift as worthy to them.

The more kindnesses a believer bestows in their present life results in more kindnesses he/she receives in the next life. Hearing that last comment made me thankful for the discipline of that particular practice, but also made me wish the whole world operated in that same manner.

Riding in the car on our way back to Shanghai, Jo Ling reviewed our itinerary for the next day. I had forgotten we were scheduled to visit a famous Buddhist Temple.

The information I was able to glean regarding the Chinese process of choosing babies for adoptive families is usually referred to as "matching" and is the subject of great amounts of analysis, thought and mystery. The legal process occurs in the "matching room" at the China Center for Adoption Affairs. Many different criteria have been suggested as the method of matching—facial features similar to prospective parents, etc., but most adoptive parents consider it God's will to have the particular child chosen for them, saying they would not disrupt the adoption, no matter what child they were

matched with, any more than they would reject a biological one.

Not a soothing thought, but on occasion babies with mild to severe health problems are denied by adoptive parents previously unaware of the child's condition. Upon learning that, I couldn't help but be reminded of the special needs children close to my heart. I was certain the kids turned away would no doubt have proven themselves more than worthy of the gift of a new family.

I remain thankful for the thousands of kindred spirits like Grace, Matt, and their children, who want to give hope to the world by unselfishly adding to their families, while simultaneously sparing the lives of so many young children. It has become apparent to me that ever-evolving kindnesses occur in many more circumstances than the tiny river-towns of China.

Buddhist priests at the Jade Buddha Temple

Chapter Seventeen

Since 6th century B.C., Buddha, the enlightened one, has had devoted followers keeping his teachings, rules of conduct, and methods for spiritual attainment. My interpretation is the journey to enlightenment leads believers to achieve inner peace and harmony in order to reach their ultimate goal...Nirvana.

I got up the nerve to ask Jo Ling if she was a follower of Buddhism, and her response was, "I'm a casual Buddhist." I left it at that, wondering if religion might have lost favor with some of the younger set.

The Jade Buddha Temple was located on an unbearably crowded street in the middle of the busy city. Shops, vendor booths and entrepreneurs were selling everything imaginable. The cacophony of blaring car horns and squealing children chasing each other belied the calm inside the temple. We entered and had to step over a two-inch thick brass threshold, twelve inches high, duly placed for signaling respect to Buddha. A throng of visitors and worshipers lined the walls as eight monks, dressed in golden-colored robes, chanted in unison. The heavy smell of incense permeated the air as it circled above the heads of each priest. Jo Ling mentioned she had only seen three "full-blown" services in her life, so I took that seriously and gave it my full attention.

Altars on all four sides of the temple displayed different characteristics of Buddha. One was sitting with arms akimbo, two standing, and one sitting with arms held high. All were made of heavy brass and laden with jewels. Living kindnesses had been placed at the feet of each Buddha, and security guards were busily gathering the donated money, and quickly stuffing each bill and coin into large cloth bags. It's my guess that particular temple was pretty solvent. Then, as we exited, I watched all of the believers depart the magnificent spectacle in what I hoped for them was an enlightened sense of radiant contentment.

Next, Jo Ling led us up a creaky staircase in an old building adjacent to the temple. We entered a huge room that appeared to be part of a warehouse. Two perfectly matching glass boxes were centered behind sectioned-off lines of rope, similar to the security entrance in a busy airport. Exquisitely carved ancient sculptures of Buddha were contained inside each framework. One was depicted as a modern-day smiling Chinese Buddha holding his big belly, but the other, thin and lying in repose, was a depiction of the true Buddha that traversed the continent from India. Each had been sculpted from pure jade and covered with an inestimable amount of cherished jewels. The sight of all the extravagance made me fairly confident the place was properly monitored by the most sophisticated security system in the world.

As I previously alluded, the communist government wreaked havoc on the temples throughout the country. In Shanghai, the same thing occurred, but in this circumstance, both jade Buddha were fortunately hidden from greedy and deadly forces. A few courageous priests had concealed their cherished prizes in two large wooden crates, and had placed them in a clandestine corner of a warehouse. I don't know if the building we toured was the original, but...ironically, a large poster of Mao was tacked to the front of both packed cases, serendipitously keeping them from harm. Yet another wondrous tidbit of Chinese history for Mae.

Everything fell into place for our trip. All of the visas arrived and the airline's reservation

system opened up with frequent flier seats for Matt and Jeremiah. Zach was looking forward to his fourth year at camp and seemed oblivious to the commotion.

Corinne was pumped about the trip, and I was even more convinced about the decision to include her. Until she was on that plane, I couldn't help but think: Corinne suffers from asthma—almost every day—and we would worry endlessly if she were not with us. She takes allergy shots every week...but once we get there, we'll probably worry she'll have to miss a few of those.

Since Corinne's the queen of homesickness, she probably wouldn't sleep a wink while her mom and the rest of us were away. Even if camp had been an option, Corinne would never think about going there alone.

Finally comforted by the resolution, I knew she'd be the greatest help for her parents as she shared with them in the care of her new baby sister.

Chapter Eighteen

For our last night in Shanghai, we decided to act on Jo Ling's advice and try the Red House for dinner.

Even though the Red House was touted as the first Western restaurant in the city, it turned out to have food that was only mediocre. And it only took one look around at the other diners to know that we were definitely the only Westerners there. Still, the expansion of our restaurant repertoire made it well worth the effort.

Having returned to our hotel in a taxi, we were just in time to secretly watch a festive wedding reception occurring on the front lawn.

We retreated to the porch, enjoyed the lively music and the warm night, and cleared our minds for the next city on our list.

Many peasants continue living hand to mouth heavily relying on grandparents to travel in search of adoptive opportunities for their babies. Occasionally, the infants are left on the steps of an institution such as a bank or reputable business, in hopes a wealthy patron may pick them up, raise them with care, and most importantly pay for their education.

Unfortunately, however, most babies are left on the steps of government-run orphanages. There the infants receive rice formula, their only sustenance, often resulting in malnutrition, a greater problem.

Safety is another issue. Since there aren't enough caregivers in the orphanages, it becomes necessary to put more than one baby in each bed, often forty beds to a room. To prevent the babies from rolling over on top of one another, the caregivers might tie one of the babies' legs to the post of the bed. With that, future physical therapy may be required, and so on and so on.

I forced myself to realize the pain of, and the conscious effort behind the grandparents' actions as they try to save the lives of their grandchildren by refusing to acquiesce to the alternative governmental mandate.

Overcome with sympathetic thoughts for Mae's family, I couldn't help but wonder, "Who are her grandparents and what kind of loss must they be feeling?"

Guilin—the city of five lakes

Chapter Nineteen

Notably a meager town—by Chinese standards—with only 750,000 inhabitants, Guilin was nestled cozily between singular pointed mountains of limestone and covered over the centuries with lush green plants and trees.

As we exited the plane, David, our first and only male guide, stood ready to take us under his wing. I happily took a backseat for an hour's ride from the airport to our new accommodations. The highways sparkled anew with tremendous government allocations. One billion dollars, in fact, had been allocated to Guilin for the Olympic preparations.

Tourism is definitely their largest commodity, but our guide led us to believe the money was given in the name of "cultural pride," not for the elevated status of the 2008 Olympiad.

David was describing some of the scheduled spots for our visit while I stared bleary-eyed out of the window at the breath-taking scenery. I noticed three weary-looking peasant women on the opposite side of the road struggling to push a large wooden two-handle cart packed to the gills with hay. As I witnessed such financial contradiction, it was difficult for me to comprehend how easily David had previously discussed the wealthy government spending in Guilin—until I honestly reminded myself of the diverse society at home.

In a short time we arrived in the center of the city and David directed the driver to drop us off at the immaculately groomed Seven Star Park. Even though Jeremiah and I secretly wished we were going straight to our new lodgings, the combination of park and gardens managed to become a savored treat. Following David as he chatted about the park's history, we stepped quietly along pampered pathways that were adjoined to luxurious flowerbeds bordered by a healthy blanket of manicured groundcover. Delicately placed against the backdrop of manmade waterfalls, fountains trickled water into shallow earthen pools filled with multi-sized Koi.

Older men, making a concerted effort to stay cool, had rolled up their t-shirts underneath their armpits and were sitting on short stools in a tiny circle as they played card games. More small gatherings of people stood under stands of trees attempting to emanate coolness but conversely made me more aware of the heat and my need to relax. Then, as we walked deeper into the garden I got a second wind, and the temperature seemed to drop.

Around the next bend in the pathway we recognized the citizens' real pride and joy—a zoo—and in the middle of the clearing sat a huge panda munching on bamboo. His fenced enclosure contained a large, glass air-conditioned cage. How envious all of the animals in the Memphis zoo would be!

David's last remark as we left the park: "The city should be receiving a second panda soon."

Grace called from Guangzhou. The three of them were riding on a bus with fifteen other families as they ventured toward the meeting place/government building that held the babies and their caregivers. No words of comfort came to mind as I listened to her quivering voice. She let me know that Corinne was busying herself by trying to help entertain some of the younger children while Matt had sparked a conversation with one of the dads he'd met in Beijing. Everyone else was nervously chatting about airplane rides, Beijing experiences, families, and anything else imaginable as they tried to maintain calmness.

I have often marveled at Grace's ability to endure heightened stress and could easily picture her quiet demeanor as she talked to me on the telephone. The circumstances instantly reminded me of yet another imminent event with her precious husband.

Nine years earlier, I drove over to Grace and Matt's home to pick up Zach. He was to spend the night with Jeremiah and me while everyone anticipated the news of Corinne's safe arrival into the world.

Grace stood stoically at the door as she watched her three-and-a-half year old son jump into our car. He had seemed to have suddenly grown up—in her eyes, at least—and would soon be a big brother.

At midnight, I found that I couldn't sleep a wink while waiting for word of the baby, although I was secretly relieved not to be at the hospital this time. My only salvations for sanity were Zach as he lay sleeping on a mattress at the foot of our bed, and the steady sound of Jeremiah's soft breathing as he slept.

At 5:30 a.m., Matt called to let me know they had had one horrible moment of touch and go—when no heartbeat was heard...then, thank God, Grace's labor continued until that magic moment occurred...the miracle of birth.

Finally, my constant prayers for strength filled with love had been answered.

Replicated Ming window in the apartment in Guilin

Chapter Twenty

Exhausted from our flight and the long walk in the park, I sensed a little disappointment in our go-getter guide when we asked him to give us some time to rest and unpack. As David settled on an hour for returning to pick us up, we arrived at a condo that had been arranged for us by Louie...who truly wanted us to experience at least one stay in a realistic Chinese family home.

The one-bedroom apartment was fairly isolated from the busy streets. David told us that Louie and his company owned the condo—convenient for him, but for us, we were out in the middle of nowhere.

Nevertheless, the efficiency was lovely. Filled with handsome Ming furniture, the door opened into a large living area with a sizeable bedroom immediately on the left, and a bathroom connected to a kitchen on the other side. An artistic circular window provided a commanding view of the extended neighborhood.

As in all of the other cities we visited, the sounds of growth continued—right outside our window. The workers were as noisy as a hive of busy bees, which made for a few censorable thoughts from me.

Acres of fields, where numerous tiny homes had previously stood, had been prepared for sites to construct several new style apartment/condominium complexes. My eyes followed the robust workforce outside of our window as they poured concrete for an enormous slab, but my heart felt a cord of dejection for the unfortunate homeowners who had most likely lost out on the monies that were being made by a handful of government-type developers.

In the next moment, I longed to be with Grace and her family and, just as abruptly, I realized my ignorance in putting our itinerary together.

Having miscalculated our timetable, we had accidentally given ourselves an extra day in Guilin, which meant one less in Guangzhou. I fully knew Louie's intentions were impeccable, as well as his desire to be thorough, so I tried my best to compel my erratic emotions to dissipate. Finally they did...somewhat.

David was twenty-four years old, short in stature, physically well-toned, and eagerly passionate about his role as tour guide. Both of us noticed he was never without his expensive briefcase and consistently acted super official while on the job. Subsequently, Jeremiah learned the reason for his self-important behavior. David's dad had become a member of the Red Guard, then had fled to the northern part of the country where he remains today. No wonder.

One of David's hobbies was following soccer. The World Cup matches occurred while we were in Guilin, and the only problem: They were aired at 2:00 A.M. Thankfully for us, his staying up half of the night never seemed to hamper David's enthusiastic style, except for an occasional catnap in the van as our driver drove us from place to place.

A fisherman with his cormorants on the lake in Guilin

The delightful food experiences of the past ten days had taken away any worry I might have sheltered about mysterious meals...until I met up with the likes of David. His favorite choice of fare was served in a revolving restaurant on the top of an old hotel (circa 1970), which not surprisingly captured a superb panoramic view of the city. It was a great marketing ploy for the local guides; plus I gathered it was fairly inexpensive.

The elevator opened up into the middle of a large dining room where we were instantly barraged by the vision of an enormous smorgasbord displayed on elongated tables connected to each other and arranged around the entire circumference of the restaurant.

I was immediately reminded of the splendid Sunday buffet that's hosted by the Arlington Hotel in downtown Hot Springs, Arkansas. They consistently present a delightful display of flavorful cheese assortments, appetizers, salads, and multiple entrees centered by a four-foot-tall ice sculpture.

With the sight of such an extraordinary amount of food, I assured myself it would be a no-brainer to pick out something suitable to my tastes. That's where I was dead wrong.

When my mind finally grasped the delicious delicacies David deemed worth pointing out (such as fish eyeballs, raw squid, bird eggs, and dark green, stringy seaweed soup), I completely lost my appetite. There was not one pseudo-normal item in my realm of likely edibles to consider. I thought, "Even back in the good ole US of A, there would be a table laden with magnificient desserts, at the very least–especially in Hot Springs–if the tables were turned."

Admittedly we had become terribly spoiled with all of our previous spreads, but unfortunately that knowledge didn't stop me from continuing to worry about the meals that were sure to follow. Then...in an instant glimmer of hope...I entertained the possibility of losing a pound or two.

On the second morning of our visit, just as I suspected, we returned to the same hotel buffet. Jeremiah and I simply ordered tea and coffee.

David, while sitting at a different table with the driver, finally noticed we had not gotten up to eat. Worriedly, he walked over and asked if we felt okay. We gently tried to explain our dilemma. Without a second's hesitation, David escorted us around the room to a sort of short-order window.

The chef was serving all types of cooked eggs, noodles and beans in what appeared to be a delicious sauce, and, a few other somewhat identifiable breakfast specialties. Feeling like idiots, we stepped right up to the window and pointed out our choices.

Even for an adventurous eater like me, breakfast turned out to be the only meal I ate for the next three days, and that included our lunch on a boat ride that same afternoon.

As we traveled down the Li River south of Guilin, I couldn't even look at what was served. Jeremiah tried to point out the fact that every local person around me seemed to enjoy whatever it was, but I happily sipped on a bottle of beer and listlessly gazed through the wide window, watching as we slowly passed by the gorgeous range of mountains.

Early the next day we departed the condo for a ski lift ride up to the top of those same mountains. My paralyzing fear of heights nearly kept me grounded until the cell phone rang. It was Grace. She was holding Mae in her arms.

Suddenly, our lift was flying through the air, and my fear ALMOST vanished as the joy of Mae's safe arrival sank into my brain. We soared through the canopy of trees into the wide-open sky, flying high enough to see the entire city of Guilin ensconced in the middle the jutting limestone that simulated giant green skyscrapers. It couldn't have been more perfect.

Having received one of the sweetest calls of my life, I knew I'd never forget the time or the unexpected place where I was sitting when I heard the touching news.

Family after family had been called forward to receive their babies. Corinne watched anxiously as she smiled and giggled at each new arrival. Finally, theirs was the last name called.

Grace, Matt, and Corinne stood ready as Mae came through the door. She was dressed in a faded Christmas t-shirt and carried by the weary caregiver from the orphanage who had ridden on the bus for five long hours holding Mae in her arms.

*Having barely heard their name, Grace gently held out her arms having already recognized the tiny face she had fallen in love with, only six **long** weeks ago.*

Folding Mae to her heart, she softly kissed each cheek and tenderly cried, "It's okay, it's okay, I'm your Mama, Mae, I'm your Mama."

Mae held on to a tiny silver necklace around Grace's neck and never looked back.

Matt had tears streaming down his face as he videoed the precious homecoming and watched Corinne wait patiently for Mae's attention. That didn't take long at all.

* From that day forward, Grace has continued to let Mae know that even though she came to them from China, she was born in Grace's heart.

What a loving comfort that enduring truth will always be for Mae.

Replica of the San Francisco Bridge on one of the lakes in Guilin

Chapter Twenty-One

Our busy day continued with a visit to one of the many tea plantations in the area. Acres and acres of bushes were showing off their multiple stages of growth. We were allowed to view the drying process, then, given a short lesson on the myriad types of tea.

Upon entering a tiny room set up for tasting, the shopkeeper gave us a sampling of some of his favorites. I was not able to read the leaves but, I certainly enjoyed all of the tasty teas.

The Li River poured into the center of Guilin creating five lakes connected to each other like a network of labyrinths. After witnessing a breath-taking sunset mirrored on the dark blue water, we enjoyed a two-hour boat ride leading us through waterways and under bridges that displayed tiny blinking lights arranged to form likenesses of the Golden Gate Bridge of San Francisco, and the famous London Bridge.

As dusk took over, we watched local fishermen in small, self-oared flatboats follow alongside our vessel using cormorants on short ropes to fish and entertain the tourists. You can bet it was a well-deserved tip time for them.

In the 1940's, when Mao took over the old communist guard, another of his harsh endeavors was implementing birth control, proclaiming there were too many mouths to feed. As the Great Leap forward progressed in the mid-1950's, Mao abandoned his ban on birth control in an effort to strengthen the forces of agricultural labor. Severe birth control was reinstated in the seventies and has

made family life in modern China unbalanced as reports conclude there are far too few women for the vast number of men. As a result, the lack of females makes more commonplace problems with women being kidnapped and/or pushed into prostitution.

Certainly not threatened by the freedoms of the West, the communist government seems to stay committed to their cause when actions taken by their people compete with ideas of loyalty to the state, especially regarding childbirth. I can only be thankful for the first year of life Mae was able to endure, and be sympathetic with others as I recall hardships my children and I lived through, and the happiness we shared simply being together.

Blessed to have been born in America where freedom of religion allows Christianity and the revered by-products, I'm thrilled with thoughts of Mae, and certain my prayers will always include the hope of a secure future for her and all of the Chinese children in harms' way.

Lobby of the White Swan Hotel

Chapter Twenty-Two

Guangzhou, the third largest city in China, is the industrial Mecca of the world. Also known for their southern Cantonese food, the city boasts 10,000 restaurants. That fact seemed incongruous to me when I learned one out of eight Chinese citizens in the province still live in abject poverty. Noting that, it was no surprise to me that tired dismal buildings and countless warehouses were all we could see on our 45-minute ride along the expressway from the airport.

The closer we got, the more anxious I became. It was worse than our arrival into the country a few short weeks ago. I kept trying to console myself by remembering Louie had made our reservations at the same hotel as the Holt Agency and the adoptive families.

When our driver finally turned the car into a secured one-way road, we wound through a dense forest of deep green flowering trees and entered through a gate that opened into the side access. The stunning five-star White Swan Hotel was nestled on a peninsula surrounded by the scenic Pearl River and clearly imparted a wondrous vision, in more ways than one.

Breathless with anticipation, I entered the front doors. It was like the trumpets at reveille; my new day had arrived. Incredulous at the number of parents at the reception area that were strolling by with their newly adopted babies, I just had to ask one of the mothers if she knew Grace. She explained that there were lots of groups booked in the White Swan, and added she was sorry, but did not know her.

There were no messages at the front desk, so we decided to try calling their room. No answer.

But there was no way I was going to our room for fear of missing them!

We roamed around the hotel and discovered a huge lobby on the second floor. At once I felt a familiar hotness behind my eyes as I spotted our precious children sitting in a cozy corner near huge windows overlooking the river.

My first thought was, "What about Mae's sense of security? Can she be strong enough for us to come close without scaring her?"

Having not revealed ourselves, we cautiously held back a moment watching the tender scene. Matt and Corinne were smiling at Grace and Mae. Grace's demeanor epitomized the happy glow of a new mother in love with her baby, as Mae lay molded on Grace's shoulder like a fine leather glove should encase an elegant hand. They both appeared relaxed, as though in a happy trance, and the closeness of the family scene was remarkably recognizable as a sense of God-given love and warmth into which Mae had already been graciously included.

Upon our approach, Corinne immediately ran up to us and unknowingly calmed me down greatly with her tight squeeze. After hugs and kisses all around, I turned toward Mae's gaze. In a few short seconds, my brain felt rigid as I realized how slowly she seemed to respond.

Previously on the telephone, Grace warned me that Mae was fragile, but the lethargy frightened me. My speedy prayer held hope it was due to the lack of proper food and stimulation in the orphanage.

I steadied myself as her soft brown eyes slowly focused on her own tiny fingers stretching out to reach mine. Timidly, I wrapped my hands around her thin delicate body and lifted her to my impatient heart, all the while humbled by her willingness that allowed me to take hold. The strange and unknown quantity that caused so many months of angst quietly dissipated as I held that exquisite China doll in my arms. Basking in the delirium, I became certain of the love I would always have to offer her. Calmly, Grace gave our reunion a little time, and then filled us in on a few of the particulars. I held tightly to Mae as Grace softly spoke.

From the moment Mae was handed to Grace, it was obvious Mae had fever. When their bus returned to the hotel, Grace and Matt had immediately taken Mae to an American clinic located on the third floor. The physician discovered she had a severe respiratory infection and immediately put Mae on antibiotics. She was responding well to the medication.

Grace added that when they visited the clinic, she found out Mae weighed only fourteen pounds, proving their theory that she was definitely the smallest child in the adoptee group. She continued to inform me further regarding the children from foster homes and their tendency to weigh more than babies coming from orphanages. Additionally, they are less likely to be sick at the time of the parental exchange, as their care is more closely regulated. The downside for them is often they suffer from anxiety issues after separating from their foster parents. As I listened intently to Grace, I learned there is no easy way for any of these beloved babies.

Forewarned by the agency prior to the trip, all of the new parents were notified they should be prepared for anything that might be needed in order to care for their babies. Consequently, most arrived armed with antibiotics, salves for severe diaper rash, powdered formula filled with vitamins, extra blankets and clothing.

Grace and Matt were definitely laden with their fair measure of provisions. Not only had other adoptive parents in Memphis warned them about different needs, but, before the school year was over, some of Grace's friends had given her a baby shower. Corinne had even thought ahead and brought some of her well-loved stuffed animals, her own favorite blanket, and a new pacifier—just for Mae.

One of the entrances to Qing Ping Market

Chapter Twenty-Three

When it came time for acquainting Mae to new foods, she timidly explored the carefully selected items placed in small piles on the tray of her high chair.

Without a tooth in her mouth, Mae thrilled her parents by gleefully attempting to sample her very first taste of Cheerios and scrambled eggs. Apparently having never held anything in her hands other than the possibility of a bottle—which was usually propped in the crib by the caregiver—it was great watching her as she learned to manipulate her fingers with the tiny pieces of food.

Incidentally, each one of us...and Corinne was certainly included...appreciated the major lack in Mae's previous diet, and were equally devastated over that fact. But fortunately we all had the presence of mind not to dwell on it.

As our visit progressed, Grace continued to keep us updated on all of the particulars about Mae, even the sad ones. Imperceptible to Jeremiah and me were night terrors, a phenomenon prevalent in babies from orphanages.

Apparently, the fretful episodes are caused by sudden strange smells, sounds, or often simply stray emotions or memories. They occur while the children are sleeping. The affected babies waken with a start, cry out with frightened screams until the feelings subside, then, take quite some time to be soothed back to sleep.

The irresolute feelings endured by so many children lingered in my mind like a dark cloud before a storm. I knew it was impossible to comprehend what struggles their new families must face in their future, but as my thoughts wearily traveled toward the probability of long sleepless nights ahead for Matt, Grace and Mae, I secretly committed myself to be close by for her long afternoon naps.

I tried to be consistently prayerful for Mae not to be affected by the sensations often connected with lifelong personal perceptions, such as a lack of self esteem and the harsher feeling—fear of abandonment. But I am somewhat relieved to know that Corinne and Zach have a remarkable sense of self-confidence, so Mae surely has more than a glimmer of hope.

Mae's new-found freedom did seem painfully fragile to me, but at the same time, I recognized what a privileged beneficiary she and I had suddenly become. Sitting in the midst of this dear family, I was able to grow stronger with the innumerable shades of emotion I encountered as I watched them try to maintain a delicate balance between themselves and their new addition. Mae's sweet need was giving all of us a sense of renewed spiritual growth and strength, with a fresh measure of pure joy. What gifts!

Our family enjoyed the rest of the morning together in the elegant hotel surroundings as the employees catered to any need. On every floor, a receptionist was present to greet each person by name upon exiting the elevators, followed by quietly stating the correct room number. The waiters and waitresses in the dining room were just as courteous as they made sure all were promptly seated and given access to the plentiful buffet. By the way, most of the food served during our stay was typically American since the hotel catered to the adoptive families.

Matt informed us the Prime Minister of China stays at the White Swan during his

visits in the province. It's my opinion that his presence must put a huge responsibility on the hotel staff, but at the same time, hands out to each employee the highest compliment of appreciation, especially since he chooses to return to the same hotel every year.

The employees seem acutely aware that an opportunity for a well-paid job should never be taken for granted, realizing if the work is not done properly, a replacement may lurk right around the next corner.

Silently I thought, "Could that behavior ever be ingrained in many of the employees back home in America that seem to be filled with feelings of entitlement? Are our country's citizens unable to apply a bit of discipline to their children and grandchildren in that regard?"

I must admit I've been guilty of the same, on occasion.

One of many delicacies in Qing Ping Market—seahorses

Chapter Twenty-Four

After lunch, the Holt Agency arranged for a special picture to be taken of all the children in Mae's group. Each child was seated on a red couch reserved for all of the adoptive occasions. Corinne smiled proudly as she watched her baby sister squirm along with fourteen other little girls. Mae was wearing the only smocked dress, one that Grace had made for Corinne when she was a baby.

Finally, the picture was snapped, wiggles and all. Later, we tromped outside dressed in bathing suits and flip-flops—Mae is now totally enthralled with that type of shoe—to enjoy a swim in one of the hotel's four pools. Grace told us Mae had taken to the water timidly at first, but by the time we arrived, she had acclimated beautifully. In all probability, Mae had never had more than a sponge bath, much less a swim.

On their first day with Mae, Corinne helped with the baby's first bath by getting in the tub and enticing Mae into the water. What a great big sister!

Jeremiah and I sat on the edge of the pool and chatted with an older, previously childless couple as they played with their new two-year-old daughter. After listening to their gentle story, we watched grateful enthusiasm and appreciation wash over them. I've never seen so many happy, thankful people in one spot.

Later that afternoon, Holt graciously included us in a boat ride along the Pearl River and afterwards, a poolside dinner back at the hotel. It was wonderful to have spent such a glorious day with so many precious families... especially ours.

Only one day was left for us to walk around the peninsula's pristine tree-lined roads. The picture perfect neighborhood had been transformed from an extension of the hotel into a tiny village with restaurants and specialty shops catering to the new adoptive families. Some of the owners pledged a portion of the money back to the orphanages in the province. Knowing about the donations made our purchases hold even more meaning.

Matt, Jeremiah and I decided to walk through the massive Qing Ping Market across the canal from the hotel. It was a little much to ask of Grace and the children, so they went back to their room for some much needed R & R.

The market area occupied a 4-mile radius of city blocks and was filled with flea market style overhangs and open-air shops that historically provided a location for locals and peasants to purchase merchandise and food for their homes or restaurants. Now tons of visitors and tourists mill around looking for bargains, too. Goods were displayed on tables, on the sidewalk, and in the middle of the street. Everything imaginable laid in wait of a sale:

dried starfish and seahorses, piles of snakeskin, strange meats, and proteins like fried crickets, dried beans and lentils, with countless more—blue jeans, t-shirts, underwear, shoes, pots and pans, and even the wonderful aroma of homemade food steaming on grills close to every curbside.

We followed Matt as he adventurously wound us through hundreds of tiny alleyways and down neighborhood sidewalks while his artist's eye busily took thousands of photos. Two hours later, Jeremiah and I gave up and headed to the closest hotel lobby—a Holiday Inn, believe it or not, right in the middle of downtown—for a beer, but not before I stepped into an antique shop and purchased ten silver cloisonné fingernail extensions for two dollars. I was certain they might have been worn by an elegant geisha in another 1940s movie—well, that's my story, and I'm sticking to it!

The next morning, I e-mailed Zach and Curt, packed for our train ride to Hong Kong, and fumed, once again, for not realizing our itinerary gave us so little time with the children. It was July 4th, Grace and Matt's anniversary, and time for us to get on with the last leg of our trip. My only consolation was the fact they were all leaving the following day.

Jeremiah kindly understood my frustration as we said our goodbyes, and gently urged me into the cab that took us to the train depot. I felt lost like a ball in tall grass and became filled with despair. "What if Mae doesn't remember me when we get home?"

The Chinese government set the standard for the Holt Agency in regard to the itineraries for the adoptive families. A 10-day stay was required—not including the mandatory 3- day visit in Beijing and the flight to Guangzhou—in the name of a visa time-limit, five days for the city and five days for the province. A wellness document was also required, combined with a release from a local doctor assuring the baby's health was good enough to travel. While in

Guangzhou, Grace and Matt were concerned Mae's condition might worsen. If her fever persisted, it was possible she wouldn't be allowed to leave the country.

View of downtown Hong Kong Island

Chapter Twenty-Six

O nce we were on our way, I forced myself to become excited about our last adventure. But, truly, after meeting our "raison d'etre," mentally the trip was over for me. We were soon lost in our own thoughts while the glistening rain pounded on the windows of the express train as it glided through the beautiful countryside.

On July 1st, 1997, Hong Kong was legally and officially returned to the Chinese people. Having not participated in the Great Leap Forward or the Cultural Revolution, financial development had easily reached the rampant stage.

The Hong Kong Harbour Plaza Hotel was on the mainland of Kowloon at a high point of the harbor directly across from the famous island. We walked from the train station with our suitcases in hand and missed the sky bridge into the main entrance of the hotel. Leading the way, I dragged Jeremiah up the down ramp meant for buses and around to the front of the hotel entrance. We looked disheveled and were definitely out of breath, but we made it without Jeremiah saying one discouraging word. What a man.

The far-reaching harbor below our hotel windows was an imposing display filled with an uncountable array of barges topped with massive containers piled high on top of each other. I considered how much business the port of Hong Kong harbor is reputed to handle and realized statistics revealed more tonnage is distributed from the depots and ports of Memphis, including the airports of southeast Memphis. Naturally, Fed Ex *does* play a part.

Once unpacked, we made a quick decision to ride the hotel van into the downtown area to get acclimated to the city before the sun went down.

The streets were packed with deferential business types and urban eclectics scurrying past as though no one else occupied the sidewalk. Multi-colored office buildings that faced the water, *fengshui*-style, were covered in blinking neon signs screaming company names, most of which had originated in the U.S.

A block away from the waterfront, the original Peninsula Hotel was hard to miss, so we decided to peek inside for a glance at the opulence. The five-star hotel resonated with a British flair as elegant displays of history lined the walls and filled the lobby. Glass-covered cases stuffed with antique silver had been placed next to formal settings of priceless furniture. Prices of drinks on the bar menu were equally exorbitant, so we chose MY only option...moving on. By the way, the namesake hotel in Beijing was far from comparable, but nevertheless remained a fantastic experience.

On the second day after their arrival in Guangzhou, Matt and Corinne decided to take an unexpected tour offered by the Holt Agency. It was an hour's bus ride out into the barren countryside for a visit to one of the many governmental orphanages.

Grace had nixed the idea right off the bat. She felt not only ill-prepared emotionally, but Mae would have to ride with them. Once that baby was put in her arms, she certainly wasn't about to leave her. Plus, her mother's natural instinct made her upset at the thought of the reaction Mae might have at seeing an orphanage. Talk about feelings of abandonment! At any rate, that point was moot.

Corinne told us about her adventure. "The bus ride took about an hour. When we arrived at the orphanage where the children lived, it looked like a hotel. It was really sad. We saw kids standing at large windows looking out at us as we got off of the bus, but the tour guide said we couldn't go in their rooms.

"We followed our guide inside and were asked to stay on one side of a huge room. There was a wall covered with white tiles with a big picture window in the middle. The wall separated the visitors' room from the babies' room. There were about twenty-five babies lying in the beds with two caregivers in the room with them. The caregivers passed only the 'favorite babies' through the big window to the visitors. You could tell they were the favorites by their chunkiness since they were well fed, and when we picked them up, they smiled.

"Also, some of the babies got to sit in rockers on the floor. You could tell which ones were used to the privilege because they rocked themselves while we played with them. The floors were dusty, there were no fans on either side of the rooms, and it was very hot. The babies were in wooden cribs that looked bare, and only two babies had blankets. The visitors were not allowed to enter the room where the babies were in cribs, and **NO** pictures."

In a field way behind the orphanage, there was a pig farm that proudly donated all of their proceeds to the orphanage.

The experience sounded like an eye-opener that gave Corinne a true sense of what her little sister had been through.

May God bless all of the babies, the older children, and all of the caregivers.

One of the many roads in Qing Ping Market

Jeremiah at the Peak Restaurant overlooking Repulse Bay

Chapter Twenty-Seven

The next day we were worn out mentally and physically, and decided to stay close to our hotel. Lunch in one of the restaurants was delicious, and the pool and spa areas were especially delightful.

With only one day left for our visit in China, the exploration of Hong Kong Island became our only agenda. Mingling with the crowds on the frantic streets, we decided to try and find an easy way to visit Hong Kong but got completely turned around. After stopping at a huge gray office-type building to ask for directions to the ferry, the receptionist explained that we had entered a YMCA housed inside the Salzbury Hotel. Surprised by that, we tucked the info away for the future—you never know—and continued our quest.

Sure enough, five minutes later we were riding on the Star Ferry headed for the formidable island. Stepping off at the dock, we followed the signs for a tour bus stop, waited a moment and climbed on.

Tree limbs hovered over the narrow roads like umbrellas as the huge vehicle traveled the streets of Hong Kong, straight up and at a dizzying speed. The driver hurriedly turned corners left and right nearly careening into small cars blocked by loaded garbage trucks, all of which were forced to back up for us!

We tried to listen as he pointed out the hotels crammed close to restaurants, and apartments crammed next to condos, plus several commercial buildings that had also been packed on top of the mountainous terrain. We passed numerous red trolley tour buses going much slower than we were—as well as cars, people, and the Happy Valley horse-racing track, looking sadly closed for the season. The bus gained momentum for the last curve, and we held our breath the rest of the way to the top of the mountain.

After numbly stepping from the bus, we riveted ourselves to a bench close by the stopping place and tried to focus our eyes on an arresting view of the waterway at the back side of the island.

The Peak Restaurant, housed in a gorgeous three-tiered glass shopping mall, was conveniently located next to our perch. Naturally for us to opt for a meal, we entered the dining area and asked for a table overlooking Repulse Bay. Our meal was marvelous, and consisted of sumptuous amounts of fresh soft-shelled crab, lightly fried, accompanied by a serving of buttered asparagus. Afterwards, as I felt a few more pounds immediately attach to my body, we rated the meal right at the top of our list, along with our first and only Peninsula Hotel feast.

Quickly tiring of the shops in the mall, we walked around the mountain precipice, snapping photos and reconnoitering for an alternative route for our return down the mountain. Obvious signage pointed us toward the entrance to a bright red tram.

Jumping on just in time, we descended the mountain in three minutes and ended up right in front of the ferry terminal. Realizing how easy that was, we were furious with ourselves for not having done our homework beforehand.

Later that evening, my mind filled with dreamy thoughts of Mae as we enjoyed a boat ride along the Hong Kong harbor. We watched the blinking lights and struggled with wrapping our minds around our three-week adventure and...last but not least...the prospect of going home.

Scads of babies remain in orphanages and foster homes all over China.

Since the time of Mae's adoption, some of the requirements for adoptive parents have changed. They are certainly not set in stone, having become familiar with the Chinese government's style of change, but the following is a list of the ones I've heard about:

Single people are no longer able to adopt.

The age limit for adoptive parents is now 30 to 49.

Adoptive parents are not allowed to be on certain prescription medications, such as those for the treatment of depression.

Adoptive parents have a body mass index restriction. To be overweight is a "no-no" in their culture.

Parents may be older if they are listed for a waiting baby, one with medical issues.

The wait time for adoptive parents is less if the child has special needs.

Downtown Hong Kong Island at night

Chapter Twenty-Eight

G race let me know that Zach returned from camp seeming a little disappointed in his two-week experience. He said it hadn't been as exciting as the previous four years had been, and his counselors weren't nearly as dynamic as all of the others.

When I came home from our trip and had a chance to see him, I attributed Zach's basic lack of energy and out-of-sorts attitude to the fact that his family had gone on a magnificent trip without him, and nearly everyone else in the family had already met Mae. As my mom often said, "His nose seemed a little out of joint," and his did.

Fortunately, it took Zach less than a week to acclimate to everything that had occurred in his absence. His good-natured humor returned, and he quickly learned his knew role was one to be savored, especially when Mae started clambering after her "big brother," making everything seem normal and comfortable once again.

Later that week, Curt and Mary came over to Grace's to meet and greet Mae. Both were instantly enamored. She eagerly hugged and kissed each of them.

One of Jeremiah's three daughters asked all of us in our blended family to come over for a cookout and, of course, to meet Mae. All of our children held out open arms for the new addition in our ever-growing family, making one of those memorable moments for Jeremiah and me. We were proud of our efforts as we watched acceptance and joy envelop everyone.

Typical of her nature, Grace decided to take a year off from teaching—simply to nurture and care for Mae. Knowing professional needs were also in order for the baby, she contacted the Tennessee Early Intervention System.

To become part of the program, each child must be a certain percentage behind or the system will not help defray the extra costs. Mae's needs for physical therapy did quantify, and she was accepted into the system. Grace was able to find capable therapists their insurance company would cover, with the overages to be met by TEIS.

Immediately, physical therapy began, and a speech therapist came on board. One of Mae's legs dragged behind her a little when she crawled. We hated to think why.

Having worked with Mae for the past year, the therapists have now been released. Mae is right on target for her age.

Grace and Mae on our Pearl River boat ride in Guangzhou

Chapter Twenty-Nine

Now fondly known as Mae Mae, our sweet baby is about to celebrate her second birthday. The tiny, frail infant I met a year ago is hardly recognizable. Her thin, brownish hair is now sparkling and black, thanks to her new formula filled with vitamins. Mae's precious little body has grown much fuller and stronger, and her arresting beauty and bubbling personality are personified by a joyous outlook. She runs, laughs, jabbers incessantly, and squeals "Bacie"—the name Zach, Corinne and Mary call me—every time I walk through their back door. As I wrap my arms around her, I'm still in awe of the feelings she's given me.

Grace returned to school teaching half-day, every day. After a short separation adjustment from her mama, Mae Mae became the darling of the mothers-day-out caregivers, charming them with her sweet smile.

She continues to be a welcomed sight in the early mornings as she lovingly greets all of Grace's teaching partners and proudly walks to her own classroom.

This wonderful carving is a prime example of Chinese art.

Chapter Thirty

The greatest news for me is my grandmother's heart has grown wiser with much more reasoning ability and much less wasted emotional energy that was previously colored by seemingly monumental difficulties. Those innumerable thoughts that held such dismal promise flew away and were replaced with a lucid and exhilarating realization. I've received one of the most phenomenal gifts of my life; the honor of watching Mae and all of my grandchildren grow in stature and knowledge as they learn how important life is for themselves, the people they care about, and others in the world.

American history played a huge part in breaking through the strong barriers of the eastern world, garnering new friendships. It's my prayer those inroads will help all mankind yearn for a greater understanding of each other, maintaining the progress that's already been made.

My personal search from the Great Wall of China to the vast harbor of Hong Kong has ended, having made our family's dangling...Red Thread...a spinning connection to the priceless gift I pray we will never live without.

Mae has permeated our hearts and given each of us an experience of wonder manifested by the power of God's unending love, changing our lives beyond all measure and imagination. My new heart gives endless thanks to my Mae Mae and her precious family for allowing me the opportunity of discovery, of sharing their journey of love, and last, but certainly not least, the breath-taking memories.

Post Script: In each city, we purchased small "happies" for Mae. When she's older we hope to share in her parents' endeavor—helping to assure that Mae receives continual knowledge of her awesome heritage and, hopefully, in preparation for when we all return for another visit to China.

Grace Braun Upshaw

happyvalley330@gmail.com

About The Cover: "The entire time of writing this book, I had a vision of what I wanted on the cover. One afternoon I helped a dear friend move from a rented condo to her son and daughter-in-law's home. We pulled ton after ton of 'treasures' from the attic. Back in one of the crevices was a Chinese picture. She handed it to me and asked if I might want it. After I stared at it in disbelief, I told her I'd love to have it. We used one small portion for the cover.

Thanks, Janet!"